Magnify

the Lord With Me

Magnify

the Lord With Me

A Collection of My Poems

DAVID RAVENHILL

OFFSPRING PUBLISHERS

Magnify the Lord With Me: A Collection of My Poems, Copyright © 2023 by David Ravenhill. All rights reserved. Cover and Interior design by C. S. Ellicott, Milk & Honey Design. No part of this publication may be reproduced, stored in a retrieval system or transmitted in any form or by any means, electronic, mechanical, photocopying, recording, or otherwise without the prior written permission of the copyright holder, except brief quotations used in a review.

My heartfelt thanks to Cheryl Sasai Ellicott for her multitalented help in the cover design, layout, typesetting and proofreading.

ISBN: 978-0-9981096-5-7
Library of Congress Control Number: 2023920445
Published by Offspring Publishers,
Siloam Springs, Arkansas USA

Printed in the United States of America
28 27 26 25 24 23 / 10 9 8 7 6 5 4 3 2 1

Contents

I Knew a Man	17
You Satisfy My Longing	18
It's Time to Celebrate	19
Place a Cry Within Me, Lord	20
Let Your Glory Be Seen Again	21
He's More Than the Wind	22
Come, Holy Spirit	23
Into Your Presence	24
The Mention of His Name	25
A Thousand Voices	26
Mighty Warrior	27
There's a Fresh Anointing	28
He Reigns	29
Lord, I'm Just a Vessel	30
We Cry Out For Your Presence	31
I Worship You	32
Detain Me, Lord	33
Abba, Father, Hear My Cry	34
I've Built the Altar	35
Be Thou My Passion, Lord	36
Everything I Need	38
You're the Gift	39
You Bore My Sin	40
Would Everybody Rise!	41
Almighty God	42
Behold the Lamb	43
He's No Longer a Babe	44
Come, Holy Spirit	45
Can You Hear Him Calling?	46
Bring Our Nation Down, Lord	47
Why Not Praise Him Now?	48
Breaking of the Bread	49
Jesus	50
We've Heard About Your Miracles	51

There's a Coming Celebration	52
That's What I Love About Him	53
We Break the Bread	54
Take Us Further	55
Some Men Seek	56
Can You Hear the Hosts of Heaven?	57
Sovereign of Creation	58
The Work of God Divine	59
Once I Was Blind	60
The Story of Amazing Grace	61
My Resting Place	62
Mountains Melt Like Wax	63
As the Prophets Foretold	64
Almighty God	65
For the Sake of Your Glory	66
You Said the Time Would Come	67
Living Bread	68
Eternity's Light	69
Lord of Battle	70
Almighty God	71
My Shepherd	72
Of Whom the World is Not Worthy	73
He Laid Aside His Glory	74
You're One of a Kind	75
I Want to Know	76
Call His Name Jesus	77
God Promised	78
Welcome the King	79
The Triumph	80
There's Only One	81
Jesus	82
Christ's First Greeting	83
A Child Was Born	84
Higher and Higher	85
Awaken My Heart	86
I Am An Addict	87
Lord, Come!	88
I Make My Boast	89
You're My Well	90

I Have No Frankincense	91
He Listens to the Sound	92
Come, Holy Spirit!	93
Oh, the Love!	94
Better Than the Blood of Abel	95
Beyond Human Understanding	96
Jesus, Our Glorious Majesty	98
God Almighty Without Equal	99
Jesus	100
Jesus Was:	101
Transcendent	102
Upon the Throne	103
Exalt His Name	104
From Every Tribe and Nation	105
Holy, Holy, Holy	106
Things Seem to be Falling Apart	107
I Can't Begin to Fathom	108
Father, You Came Running	109
I Saw His Arms Extended	110
I Tried to No Avail	111
Everything We Need, You Are	112
Amazing Grace	113
The Greatest Gift	114
Worthy is the Lamb	116
In Honor of the King	117
Join Us	118
We Stand in Awe	119
Pursue Your Foes	120
From North and South	121
There's Only One Reason	122
Trinity	123
To Him Alone	124
God Almighty	125
In Your Presence	126
He's the King	127
Awesome King	128
Abba, Father!	129
I Make My Boast	130
Manifest Yourself to Us	131

Condemned to Die	132
God of Nations	133
To Christ Our King	134
God's Priceless Gift	135
Another Conference	136
Let This Cup Pass	137
We Serve Notice	138
One Day	139
Thank You	140
You Are the One	141
The Ultimate King	142
The Place Where Your Glory Dwells	143
I Stand in Fascination	144
Amazing Grace	145
You Make the Sun	146
They Crucified God's Only Son	147
Forbidden to Enter	148
I Came to Fulfill	149
When You've Tried Every High	150
The King of Love	151
From Every Tribe and Nation	152
Born to Die	153
Almighty God	154
A Glorious Bride	155
The Bride & Groom	159
Father or G_d	160
Then I Awoke	161
The Fungus Among Us	162
Left or Lost?	163
A Fish Tale	164
Sometimes We Get Offended	165
Can a Horse Change Into	166
When Will it All End?	168
The Date	170

O, MAGNIFY THE LORD *WITH* ME AND LET US EXALT HIS NAME *TOGETHER.*

PSALM 34:3

Introduction

Fires are both delightful as well as devastating. In the case of my father, the latter proved true. In 1951, while ministering for A.W. Tozer in Chicago, his life was forever changed.

He and his good Irish friend Tom Haire, who was travelling with my father at that time, were staying in the Norwood Hotel, on the fourth floor. Around 3:00 a.m. fire broke out; it quickly engulfed the stairways, leaving no possibility of escape. My father was able to assist his friend Tom, who was almost twice his age; he helped him to an open window where he proceeded to push him to the ground below. My father then jumped—breaking both his back and leg in three places, as well as smashing his feet.

Miraculously, before hitting the sidewalk below, my father heard the words of the Psalmist:

> *"YOU SHALL NOT DIE, BUT LIVE AND DECLARE THE WORKS OF THE LORD" (PSALM 118:17)*

While Tom had fewer injuries, my father had months of recovery and rehabilitation ahead of him. While lying on his hospital bed in a cast restricting his mobility, he found himself asking God: "Why?" *Why was he in this situation?* His ministry in America was being well received—yet now he was unable to even pick up his Bible, let alone preach! While he was questioning his circumstances and asking himself, *What use am I now?* he heard the Lord speaking to his heart:

YOU CAN LEARN TO WORSHIP.

I'm convinced this marked a major milestone in my father's life and ministry.

During his hospital stay in Chicago, prior to being flown back to our home in Oldham, England, my father and A. W. Tozer became friends. Tozer had told my father he was free to drop by his office anytime he was in the Chicago area.

Following a prolonged period of recovery, my father finally returned to full time itinerant ministry. He tells the story of how one afternoon he did indeed stop by to see his good friend—or to use Tozer's words: "Drop by and let your hair down," which was Tozer's way of saying, *let's be real with each other.* On the occasion of this visit, Tozer related how he had arrived at his office that morning and decided he needed to pray before launching into his daily tasks. My father, without realizing it, had interrupted Tozer's prayer time. Tozer told my father that, when my father had arrived at his office, he had not even begun to pray yet; he'd simply been lost in worship. Keep in mind that this was *well after noon.*

Why am I telling you this story? Because it goes to the very root of who A.W. Tozer really was. Most people know Tozer for his numerous writings and sermons, but Tozer was a man who knew his God in a way that few do. For hours he would find himself caught up in the awesome majesty and splendor of God's holiness. His mind would try to fathom the vastness of God's grace, power, wisdom, and mercy. Or he would find himself reveling in God's creative genius as he contemplated the vastness of the universe.

Worship is our greatest privilege and highest calling. Long after this world has been consumed by fire and replaced with a new heaven and new earth, we will still have the eternal honor of worshipping our glorious Savior and King, Jesus.

Worship is, without question, our number one priority. God is to have first place in everything we do. Worship stems from not only recognizing who God is, but also from what He has done for us. Jesus made it clear to Simon the Pharisee that, "He who has been forgiven much will love much." Perhaps for many of us we need a fresh revelation of all we have been forgiven from. Only then, like the leper who Jesus cleansed, can we return and truly worship Him for all he has done for us.

In my daily quiet times, I try to follow the Psalmist admonition to, "Enter His gates with thanksgiving and come into His courts with praise." One old song reminds us to "Count your blessings, name them one by one…" Invariably after recalling God blessings, goodness, faithfulness, provision and protection, I often find myself with a spontaneous rhyme I sing back to the Lord. After all, aren't we exhorted to "Sing and make melody in our hearts to the Lord?"

What you're holding in your hands are a variety of poetic *songs* really; poems that invariably began during my own times of worship. I certainly don't claim to be a Poet Laureate, and I even hesitate to call them *poems*. I prefer to just call them *rhymes*. My hope in publishing them is that they will inspire you to reflect again on some aspect of God's awesomeness, power, and beauty. So often we rush through our times with the Lord and fail to "sup with Him" as He desires us to. Many have lost the art of meditation, not only on God's Word, but sadly, on God Himself.

Martin Luther taught his children to read the Bible as though they were looking for apples. "First, I shake the whole apple tree, that the ripest might fall. Then I climb the tree and shake each limb, and then each branch, and then each twig—and then I look under each leaf."

In the same manner that Luther instructed his children to read the Bible, we too should apply that diligence in our own approach to God's Word. It could well be that in looking under that last leaf we'll glimpse something life transforming that would be completely overlooked by the casual reader.

These songs/poems were not written for the speed-reader, but for the *meditator*. I trust they will inspire, teach, and (more than anything) help you to MAGNIFY the Lord with me.

—David Ravenhill, 2023

Poems to Ponder

I Knew a Man

I knew a man who gave his life to see revival fire.
He prayed by day, he prayed by night, to birth this one desire.
He had but one obsession: to see a glorious bride
Arrayed in spotless purity brought to her Bridegroom's side.

His power while in the pulpit was matched by very few,
And yet he loved the closet, there with the God he knew.
While others strove for man's applause, for fortune, and for fame,
He had but one ambition: to exalt his Master's name.

For eighty-seven years he lived, just for eternity;
A man of faith and wisdom and true humility.
He knew one day he'd have to stand before God's judgment seat,
And so he ran to win the prize, his mission to complete.

The fortune that he left behind was not in stocks or gold,
But lives transformed and challenged, their stories yet untold.
Life has no greater privilege than this that I have had:
Of knowing this great man of God and having him as Dad.

(Written at the bedside of my dying father, Leonard Ravenhill)

You Satisfy My Longing

You satisfy my longing;
Silver and gold can't compare.
Riches or fame, or earthly acclaim,
Cannot your glory share.

Jesus, desire of all nations,
Awesome Redeemer and King,
You are my life; you are my joy;
You are my everything.

It's Time to Celebrate

It's time to celebrate
The victory of the Lamb;
The Son of God our Savior King,
The glorious great "I Am."

Through death He crushed the serpent's head
And made the demons cower,
And by His resurrection
Sin's grip has lost its power.

His power has no limits;
His kingdom has no end.
Creator of the universe,
And yet to me a friend.

Place a Cry Within Me, Lord

Place a cry within me, Lord,
One of deep desire.
Put a longing in my heart
For purifying fire; for purifying fire.

Come, Almighty Spirit.
Like a river flow;
Fill me with your Spirit.
Lord, it's you I long to know.

Place a cry within me, Lord,
One of deep desire.
Put a longing in my heart
For purifying fire; for purifying fire.

Come, Almighty Spirit.
Like a river flow;
Fill me with your presence.
Lord, it's you I long to know.

Lord, it's you I long to know.

Let Your Glory Be Seen Again

We lift our voices, our cry of desperation;
We long that you would come and take your place.
We need, O God, a mighty visitation
Where all would pale before your holy face.

Come, Lord, we pray; commence this restoration
Where all you've purposed will at last be known
And men from every kindred, creed, and nation
Will bow before the Lamb upon the throne.

Let nothing, Lord, eclipse this full expression
Where all your glory will at last be seen,
And this would be our treasured one possession:
The world would say, "With Jesus they have been."

Lord, in this final day and dispensation,
You promised, Father, that your church would be
Arrayed with glory greater than the former;
Your kingdom manifest for all to see.

Let your glory be seen again!
Let your glory be seen again!
In this final generation
Grant us Lord a visitation,
And let your glory be seen again!

He's More Than the Wind

He's more than the wind;
He's more than the rain.
He's more than a dove;
He's more than a flame.

He's more than just oil or a river to me.
He's a person more real than any you see.
So come, Holy Spirit; I welcome you here
To comfort, convict, to counsel and cheer.

Come, Divine Helper,
And my teacher be.
Come glorify Jesus;
Reveal Him to me.

Come, Holy Spirit

Come, Holy Spirit;
Come here today.
Come, Holy Spirit;
Come have your way.

Come as the wind;
Come as the rain;
Come, Holy Spirit;
Revive us again.

Come as the fire;
Come purify;
Come, Holy Spirit;
Answer our cry.

Into Your Presence

I come into your presence,
Drawn by your grace alone,
And kneel in adoration
Before your glorious throne.

And as I bow in worship,
Before your Majesty,
There's nothing left for me to do
But give my life to thee.

The Mention of His Name

The mention of His name
Can calm the raging sea.
The mention of His name
Can set the captive free.

The mention of His name
Can cause the blind to see.
The mention of His name
Means everything to me.

A Thousand Voices

If I had a thousand voices,
I'd lift them all to you
In gratitude for all you've done
And all you've brought me through.

For by your love and mercy,
And solely by your grace,.
I stand here now before you
As friends stand face to face

To you I give my worship,
All that I am I bring;
I lay my life before you,
My Savior, friend and King.

Mighty Warrior

Who is this mighty warrior?
Who is this one who rides
In might and power and majesty
Triumphant through the skies?

He is the King of battle;
Great captain of the hosts.
Our undefeated warrior;
Of victories He boasts.

This ruler of the nations
Is Jesus Christ our King.
Our Lord mighty in battle.
To Him our praise we bring.

All hail to God the Father.
All hail to God the Son.
All hail to God the Spirit.
All hail eternal One.

There's a Fresh Anointing

There's a fresh anointing
Resting in this place.
Signs and wonders happening;
Mighty works of grace.

Come, Almighty Spirit.
Jesus glorify!
Lord, increase your presence.
"More, Lord!" is my cry.

He Reigns

He reigns over the nations.
He reigns over the sea.
He reigns throughout the universe.
Lord, come and reign in me.

He speaks and kingdoms rise.
He speaks and kingdoms fall.
He's the Alpha and Omega,
The sovereign Lord of all.

Lord, I'm Just a Vessel

Lord, I'm just a vessel
Made of common clay.
And without your presence,
I will stay that way.

Spirit of Jehovah,
Let this vessel be
Filled to overflowing.
Live your life through me.

Lord, I'm just a vessel
Made of common clay.
Let the world take notice:
You have come to stay.

Let them see your glory.
Let them see your power.
Pour your Spirit through me
In this final hour.

We Cry Out For Your Presence

Lord, we cry out for your presence.
Nothing else will satisfy.
See our longing, hear our pleading;
Come and answer our heart's cry.

Mountains melt, Lord, at your presence.
Nations tremble when you come.
Lame men walk and blind eyes open;
Demons cry out: "You're God's Son!"

Lord, we need a visitation.
Rend the heavens; touch our land.
All's in vain without your presence.
Help us, Lord. Stretch forth your hand.

I Worship You

I worship you, the Son of God most holy.
I worship you, the Lamb upon the throne.
I worship you, for you are great and mighty.
And of your love to us you have made known.

For you are king and ruler of the nations;
The Prince of Peace; the Rose of Sharon fair;
The altogether lovely one. We praise you,
For you are life, and of your life we share.

Detain Me, Lord

Detain me, Lord, by your Spirit.
Never let me go.
Captivate me with your presence.
It's you I long to know.

Let your divine aroma
Permeate my heart.
Nothing but your fragrance
Let my life impart.

Abba, Father, Hear My Cry

Abba, Father!
Hear my cry
For more and more
Of you.

You said if I
Asked for bread
You'd not give
A stone instead.

And to your Word
I know you will be true.
So here I stand
With open hand.

Your Spirit I desire.
Come heavenly flame,
In Jesus name,
And set my heart on fire.

I've Built the Altar

I've built the altar;
Lord, send the flame.
I'll be the sacrifice
Unto your name.

Come, Holy Spirit;
Consume me now.
Lord, in your presence
I make this vow.

Nothing but you, Lord,
Do I desire.
Your glory only;
My one desire.

Be Thou My Passion, Lord

Be thou my passion, Lord, my one desire.
Kindle afresh in me your holy fire.
Consume to ashes all plans save thine own.
King of Creation, make my heart your throne.

Sovereign of Sovereigns, let your kingdom come
As is in heaven; let your will be done
Till every nation has heard of your name;
Jesus Almighty, the Lamb who was slain.

Great Master Potter, by thy grace alone
This once marred vessel has become your home.
Lifting me up out of sin's *mirey* clay,
You placed your Spirit within me to stay.

Be thou my anchor through life's raging storm.
Speak to the tempest and let there be calm.
Captain, great Captain, now my pilot be;
Trusting and resting my faith is in thee.

Christ, be my first love, my one true delight.
Naught else my focus by day or by night.
Great Rock of Ages, so steadfast and sure,
My firm foundation and oh so much more!

Mighty in battle, now my victor be.
Death has no power since you hold the key.
Mindful forever when facing my foes:
The grave is empty; from it you arose.

One day in heaven your face, Lord, I'll see.
No greater motive can there ever be.
Be thou my passion from now until then.
Thine be the glory, forever, amen.

(TUNE: Be Thou My Vision)

Everything I Need

Everything I need, you are.
Everything you are, I need.
You alone are my desire.
For your presence, Lord, I plead.

More of you and less of me.
Not my will, but yours be done.
Holy Spirit, have your way.
Let my heart and yours be one.

You're the Gift

You're the gift that keeps on giving.
You're the reason for my living.
You're my passion; you're my one desire.
Jesus, you have set my heart on fire!

All-consuming purifier,
Cleanse me, fill me; take me higher.
Jesus, all I want is more of you.
Jesus, all I want is more of you.

You Bore My Sin

You bore my sin.
You bore my shame.
You bore my sickness.
You bore my pain.

You took the curse
When nailed to the tree,
Releasing God's grace
And mercy to me.

No greater love
Has ever been shown;
No greater power
The cross to the throne.

No greater name
Will there ever be
Than Jesus, God's son,
Our great Majesty.

Would Everybody Rise!

Would everybody rise
In honor of the King!
His Royal Majesty is here,
The Lord of everything.

The one who made the heavens,
The earth, the sky, and sea
Is standing here among us
In all his majesty!

We welcome you, Lord Jesus,
Our great and glorious King.
You gave your life to save us;
Your praise we'll ever sing!

To you alone be glory;
To you alone be praise.
We stand in awe before you,
The King of endless days.

Almighty God

Almighty God, Creator,
Ruler of everything,
We come into your presence
Our great and glorious King.

We come to magnify you,
The Lion and the Lamb.
You shed your blood,
Then took the keys
of death and rose again.

No other name is worthy.
Jesus, to you alone
We bow in adoration
In thanks before your throne.

Behold the Lamb

Behold the Lamb,
No longer crucified;
Now risen, glorified,
He reigns eternally.

In awesome majesty
His kingdom will increase.
He is the Prince of Peace,
The coming King.

Who is this risen Lamb?
Jesus the son of man;
Clothed in humility
And yet divinity.

Creation testifies;
Only the fool denies
That He is God.

He's No Longer a Babe

He's no longer a babe in a manger,
Just a figure from history.
He's no longer a lowly carpenter
Or a teacher from Galilee.

He's no longer nailed to a Roman cross
As God's sacrificial Lamb.
But He's risen and lives forevermore,
The glorious great "I Am."

Today he reigns as King of kings.
But the greater mystery
Is that Jesus Christ, the Son of God,
Is the One who lives in me.

Come, Holy Spirit

Unhindered, unfettered, unscripted,
And uncontrolled by man;
Come, Holy Spirit, and have your way.
Work out your glorious plan.

Blow like the wind; flow like oil;
Burn like fire, we pray.
Come, gentle dove of heaven,
Fall like the rain today.

Can You Hear Him Calling?

Can you hear Him calling,
Calling: "Come away!
Forget the worries of the past,
The cares of yesterday!

Now, turn your gaze upon Me.
Trust, don't be afraid.
I am God Almighty,
The conqueror of the grave!

I hold all things together;
They're under my command.
There is no need to worry.
Reach out and take My hand."

Bring Our Nation Down, Lord

Bring our nation down, Lord,
Bring her down.
Bring our nation down, Lord,
Bring her down.
Down upon her knees
Till she does as you please.
Bring our nation down, Lord,
Bring her down.

Raise our nation up, Lord,
Raise her up.
Raise our nation up, Lord,
Raise her up.
Clothed in humility
For all the world to see.
Raise our nation up, Lord,
Raise her up.

Why Not Praise Him Now?

We see the threat of Islam
Advancing far and wide.
We see the gay agenda
Increase on every side.

The liberal politicians
Are fighting for their cause,
And everywhere we turn we see
The breaking of God's laws.

But there's one thing for certain
One day we're going to see:
God's glory covering the earth
As waters do the sea.

Then all man's futile scheming
Will fail and be no more,
And Jesus Christ will triumph,
His kingdom to restore.

And every eye will see Him,
And every knee will bow;
And every tongue will praise Him.
So why not praise Him now?

Breaking of the Bread

Make yourself known
In the breaking of the bread.
Make yourself known
As risen from the dead.

Show us your glory,
Your majesty,
All conquering Savior;
Reveal yourself to me.

As with the bread, Lord,
So with the wine;
This is the symbol
Of your blood divine.

Your life poured out, Lord,
To cleanse us from sin;
Our bodies your temple
For you to dwell in.

This cup declares, Lord,
The battle is done;
Satan's defeated
And Jesus has won.

Now He's ascended
Forever to reign,
And this cup reminds us
There's power in His name!

Jesus

When I hear the sounds of heaven
Blend in perfect harmony
With all of God's creation
In one vast symphony;

When the roaring of the oceans
And the rustling of the leaves
Join the thunder of the heavens
With the buzzing of the bees;

When men from every nation
Add their voice in adoration,
There's no greater proclamation
Or more glorious celebration
Than the final coronation
Of our King:
Jesus.

We've Heard About Your Miracles

We've heard about your miracles
And mighty deeds of old.
The stories of your awesome power
Forever have been told.
Yet every time I hear them
I cannot help but pray
For them to be repeated
Throughout your church today.

Arise, O God, among us!
Stretch forth your mighty hand,
And demonstrate your power
Across our needy land.
Expose all other rivals;
Reveal your majesty
Till every foe is vanquished
And every captive free.

For the sake of the nations;
For the sake of your name;
Lord, show us your glory.
Empower us again.
Arise, Lord, among us!
Your presence we need.
There's no other answer.
For you, Lord, we plead.

There's a Coming Celebration

There's a coming celebration,
Like the world has never known,
When those from every nation
Will gather around God's throne.

They'll lift their voice in worship,
Singing *Worthy is the Lamb,*
And praise the name of Jesus,
Son of God and Son of Man.

But we don't have to wait until
That great and glorious day.
But we can lift our voices now
And praise Him everyday.

He's the Alpha and Omega;
He's the Lion and the Lamb;
He's the mighty Rock of Ages,
Forever the "I Am."

He the Author of Creation;
He's our great and glorious King.
He's our Savior and our shepherd;
He's our all, our everything.

That's What I Love About Him

That's what I love about Him,
Jesus the son of God;
Creator of the universe,
Left heaven to walk this sod.
That's what I love about Him,
That he, God's perfect Lamb,
Would shed his blood, the Son of God,
For me, a sinful man.

That's what I love about Him;
Death could not hold its prey.
He triumphed over death and hell,
Then rose on the third day.
That's what I love about Him;
He's coming back again
As King of kings and Lord of lords,
Forever more to reign.

That's what I love about Him;
For all eternity
I never will forget His love
And all He's done for me.
That's what I love about Him.

We Break the Bread

We break the bread;
We take the wine,
Remembering your life divine.
The blood you shed,
The price you paid,
Your passion and the empty grave.

We celebrate your victory
And triumph o'er the enemy.
And with these emblems
We proclaim
That you'll return
To earth again.

Take Us Further

Take us further,
Take us deeper
Than we have ever been.
Take us past the world of sight
Into the realm of the unseen.
And there by faith appropriate
The things we cannot see
And call the things which are not
Into reality.
Take us further.

Eye has not seen,
Ear has not heard
The things God has in store
For those who love His presence,
For those who thirst for more.
Take us deeper.

Some Men Seek ...

Some men seek for knowledge.
Some men seek for gold.
Some men seek for wisdom;
Some for works of old.

Men have sought to find the source
Of life's great mystery.
Some have travelled into space,
While others search the sea.

Still others look through microscopes
In search of some lost clue,
While others gaze through telescopes
In search of something new.

But I have found the treasure
That others seek to find,
A treasure that surpasses
Everything they had in mind.

Yes, I have found the source of life;
It's simple—so can you.
Become just like a child again
And then you'll understand
That God's the source of life, my friend.
Find Him; you'll understand.

Can You Hear the Hosts of Heaven?

Can you hear the hosts of heaven
As they sing their one refrain?
Holy, holy, holy!
They sing time and time again.
They exalt the name of Jesus
Singing, *Worthy is the Lamb.*
He's their one supreme obsession,
Jesus Christ the great "I Am."
There around His throne of glory
They all sing incessantly,
Holy, holy, holy!
To the Lamb of Calvary.

He's our rock and our redeemer;
He's our shield and hiding place.
He's our shepherd, He's our healer;
King of every tribe and race.
So, let's join the hosts of heaven
As they worship Christ our King,
The one who died and shed His blood
Then rose o'er everything.
Seated now above all powers
And all authority
Is Jesus Christ the Lamb of God,
Our awesome Majesty.

Sovereign of Creation

Sovereign of creation,
Jesus our majesty,
You left your throne in glory
To pay sin's penalty.

You satisfied God's justice;
Defeated death's domain;
Poured out your grace upon us;
How awesome is your name.

Ruler of the nations,
Your throne knows no defeat.
Your enemies like ashes
Lay powerless at your feet.

You raise up kings and kingdoms,
Decree their rise and fall;
You are the Lord, Almighty God,
The ruler over all.

The Work of God Divine

The God of heaven thunders, His zeal aroused for war.
The host of heaven follow, with tens of thousands more.
He stores the hail, the wind, the snow—His weapons for the fight.
It matters not how great the foe; He puts them all to flight.

He rules both kings and kingdoms, decrees their rise and fall.
Through righteousness exalted; by wickedness they fall.
But there is One, His chosen—the apple of His eye—
That He has promised to defend; He will not let them die.

Though they may strive against Him, He's faithful to His word.
All those who rise against her, will perish by the sword.
Oh, Israel Oh, Israel, I will not let you go.
The price I paid to save you, no man will ever know.

The time is near to lift the veil and cause your eyes to see
Jesus your great Messiah King, who shed His blood for thee.
Then all the world will see you grafted back into the vine,
Arrayed in robes of righteousness, the work of God divine.

Jerusalem, Jerusalem!
The nations will implore.
Teach us the ways of Zion,
Your God let us adore!

Once I Was Blind

Once I was blind, but now I see!
A captive once, but now I'm free!
Jesus, your blood has cleansed my past.
No condemnation; free at last.

Where sin abounds, your grace excels.
Where darkness reigned, your Spirit dwells.
No more alone, now to the end,
My Lord, my King—my faithful friend.

The Story of Amazing Grace

I love to tell the story
Of God's amazing grace,
How He, the King of glory,
Came down to take my place.

He satisfied God's justice
By dying on a tree,
So I could know His mercy,
From prison be set free.

No more an orphaned beggar,
But now a child of God.
I'll live with Him forever,
Jesus the Son of God.

My Resting Place

You are my home; my resting place;
My peace, my joy, my righteousness.
By day or night, where're I roam,
You are my resting place, my home.

No fear of man
Or demon power
Can break your love
Or make me cower.

No height or depth or thing unseen
Can separate or come between.
Jesus, you are my resting place,
My source of life, my happiness.

Mountains Melt Like Wax

Mountains melt like wax before His presence.
Nations rise and fall at His decree.
By His word alone He made the heavens,
Flung the stars in place for all to see.

Holy is your name, Lord God Almighty.
Awesome are the deeds that you have done.
But by far your greatest demonstration
Came to us through Jesus Christ your son.

God-made-flesh, and then made sin, for all men.
Oh, the marvel of this mystery:
Why the God of all creation's glory
Would send His son to die for one like me.

Abba Father, you alone are worthy!
Thine the kingdom, power, and majesty.
From the heart of your redeemed creation,
I'll give you the praise eternally.

As the Prophets Foretold

I can hear the rain falling,
As the prophets foretold;
A mighty outpouring
On the young and the old.

There's a river that's rising,
Bringing life where it flows;
Cleansing and healing
While destroying its foes.

I can hear the rain falling,
As the prophets foretold;
A mighty outpouring
On the young and the old.

Sons and daughters declaring,
Thus saith the Lord;
Great signs and great wonders
Fulfilling His Word.

Almighty God

Almighty God, Creator;
Ruler of everything,
I come into your presence,
My great and glorious King.

I come to magnify you,
The Lion and the Lamb.
You shed your blood,
Then took the keys of death
And rose again.

No other name is worthy.
Jesus, to you alone
I bow in adoration,
In thanks before your throne.

For the Sake of Your Glory

For the sake of your glory;
For the sake of your name;
For the sake of your kingdom,
Lord, send us your rain!
Let your river of mercy
And your river of grace
Flow out to the nations,
Every tribe every race.

Lord, arise like the dawning,
Fill the earth with your light!
Let the powers of darkness
Know the strength of your might.
Turn the hearts of the nations
To their Savior and King.
Then united in worship
We'll all stand and sing.

Thank you, Lord, for your mercy!
Thank you, Lord, for your grace!
By your blood you've redeemed us;
Made us one chosen race.
Unto you be the glory!
Unto you be the praise!
Both now and forever,
O, Ancient of Days.

You Said the Time Would Come

You said the time would come
When all would see the day
That all the world's great kingdoms
Would be like iron and clay.

Then you, the King of Heaven,
Would usher in your plan,
Establishing a kingdom
Greater than that of man.

A kingdom of such power
The world has never seen.
A kingdom that will crush all else
As though they'd never been.

No weapon formed against you
Will prosper in the day,
For you alone, Lord Jesus Christ,
Will rule and have your way.

For those of us who know you, Lord,
That day will glorious be—
When you who died upon the cross
Will reign in majesty.

Living Bread

You can starve to death
While reading a book
On bread.
God, open up our eyes—make us to realize:
Without your Spirit, Lord, your Word
Is dead!

Yes, we can memorize; analyze and theorize
And join the ranks of scribe
Or Pharisee.
They crucified instead the One of whom they read
Who came to give them life
And liberty.

Spirit of Truth, revive! Come make my heart alive
That I might feast on you,
The living bread.
Beyond the written word, Lord, let my heart be stirred
By Him who rose triumphant
From the dead.

Eternity's Light

Lord, help me live in eternity's light.
Teach me to number my days.
Help me to walk true to your word.
Show me the truth of your ways.

Tell me what brings you pleasure.
Lord, place your fear in me.
Above all else, Lord, fill my heart
With a burning love for thee!

Lord of Battle

Can you hear Him laughing
From His throne above?
Awesome is His power;
Tender is His love.

He's Alpha and Omega,
The sovereign Lord of man.
Great ruler of the nations,
No man can thwart His plan.

Kings with all their armies
Cannot alter His decree.
He's the mighty Lord of Battle,
And He's everything to me.

Almighty God

Almighty God, creator and redeemer,
We stand in awe of your great majesty!
The heavens declare your glory like no other.
Your beauty's seen across the earth and sea.

You sit enthroned in power and in splendor;
Your might's unequaled, without rivalry.
You word alone is absolute and final.
No man can question your authority.

All principalities, all thrones and powers,
Are subject to your righteous sovereignty.
No other king is worthy of such honor.
No other king can match your purity.
We lift our hearts unto your name in worship
For you reached down in love to even me.

My Shepherd

He is my King,
My shepherd guide.
My every need
His hands provide.

He makes me lie
In pastures green,
By quiet waters
So serene.

Restores my soul
When it's been stressed
And guides in paths
Of righteousness.

For His name's sake when facing death,
I do not fear; He is always near.
His rod and staff they comfort me.
Before my foes I dine with glee.

His holy oil anoints my head.
His blessings all around me spread.
Goodness and mercy follow me,
A promise He will guarantee.

And I shall dwell
Forevermore
Inside His house,
Within His door.

Of Whom the World is Not Worthy

They stand accused of loving God, believing in His Word.
Arrested and imprisoned, their cries will go unheard.
Deprived of food and family, they suffer day by day.
The world ignores their presence;
The church forgets to pray.

While thousands sit in prison cells, tortured, filled with pain,
Still others groan in rebel bands—their minds almost insane.
Some hide away in forests, their homes destroyed by fire
And pray for God's protection:
O, God, come take us higher!

Yes, God sees each and every one—and calls us all to pray
As though in prison with them experiencing "their way."
Lord God of Hosts, we lift our voice for your suffering saints.
Grant them your grace for everyday;
Revive the one who faints.

O God, the world's not worthy
Of these, your suffering throng.
May they inspire the rest of us
To stand, firm, tall and strong.

He Laid Aside His Glory

He laid aside His glory
And His great majesty
To wear a crown of thorns
And to be nailed upon a tree.

Excruciating pain he bore,
That day on Calvary.
He took the sins of all the world
That we might be set free.

Eternal God, Almighty King,
Why would you leave your throne
And come into the world you made
Rejected by your own?

I still cannot believe
That you, the great "I Am,"
Would take our place upon the cross,
The sacrificial Lamb.

What can I say or do
For all you've done for me?
My life is not my own;
Your blood has purchased me.

You're One of a Kind

You're one of a kind and the kindest one.
You're one with the Father, yet Jesus the Son.

Born of a virgin, my Savior to be,
Rejected and crucified—nailed to a tree!

Then taken and buried, no longer a threat.
But God wasn't through; He hadn't finished yet.

Three days were completed, just as He said,
Then up from the grave He rose from the dead!

I'll say it again—I know you'll not mind:
There's no one like Jesus! He's one of a kind.

There's no one like you; there's no one like you.
I've searched the world over, and I know that it's true.

Crucified, then glorified; now here to stay.
A Savior for all, for there's no other way.

I'll say it again—I know you'll not mind:
There's no one like Jesus! He's one of a kind.

I Want to Know

I want to know,
I want to understand,
The mystery of your ways;
The power of your hand.

I want to see
Beyond the realm of sight,
To know the truth—
Discern what's wrong or right.

To live in time,
Yet for eternity;
No more for self,
But wholly, Lord, for thee.

To hear your voice,
Your Spirit's gentle plea;
To call you friend
Means everything to me.

Call His Name Jesus

Call His name Jesus
Call His name Lord
Call His name Savior
The Living Word

Call His name Healer
Call His name King
Call His name Master
Of everything

Call His name Lion
Call His name Lamb
Call His name Awesome
The Great I Am

Call His name Wisdom
Call His name Love
Call His name Mercy
Sent from above

Call His name Holy
Call His name True
Call His name Faithful
His promise to you

God Promised

God promised to send us a Savior,
The seed to crush Satan's domain.
And true to the word of His promise,
In God's perfect timing He came.

He came to His own, but they shunned Him.
Despised and rejected was He.
They chose for themselves Barabbas
And crucified Christ on a tree.

Convinced they had silenced forever
The one who was mighty to save.
But true to the word of His promise,
The third day He rose from the grave!

The powers of darkness all trembled.
Defeated, they flee at His name.
Yes, Jesus—God's Lamb—our Redeemer,
Now and forever will reign!

Welcome the King

Make way for the King of Glory!
Mighty in battle is He.
So fling wide the gates, and open the doors.
Let's welcome His Majesty!

Jesus, Almighty Creator,
Your awesome presence we crave.
Show us your power and glory.
Heal, Lord, deliver and save!

Lord, be enthroned in our praises.
Stretch forth your scepter and reign.
Let every foe your power know;
Mighty the Lamb that was slain!

Jesus, you bore all our sorrows;
Carried our sin and our shame.
You promised to be where two or three
Were gathered in your name.

So welcome, great King of Glory,
Awesome in power and might!
We worship and adore you
All through the day and night.

The Triumph

See our King in regal triumph
Marching through the realms of time?
Trumpets blazing, cymbals clashing,
Banners raised—line after line!

Following Him, His blood-bought army;
Saints and angels join the throng.
Voices raised in songs of triumph;
Christ alone their theme and song.

Captives taken in the fray
March in chains, His kingdom's prey.
Priests with censers swinging follow
As their fragrance fills the air.

Life to some, but death for others
Who His kingdom's claim would dare.
Hail Almighty, King Eternal!
Hail, our great triumphant Lamb!

You alone have won the battle;
Naught could thwart your glorious plan.

There's Only One

There's only one Creator,
One Ruler over all.
There's only one Redeemer,
God's answer for man's fall.

There's only one Deliverer
Who sets the captives free.
There's only one who paid the price
And died on Calvary.

Jesus, you're the answer
For man's body, mind, and soul.
You are God Almighty;
You came to make us whole.

So we lift our voice in worship
Crying, "Worthy is the Lamb!"
For you alone deserve the praise,
Our King, the great "I Am."

Jesus

He created the world he came into
And the sea that He walked upon.
He formed the eyes that He opened
And the donkey He rode upon.
There was never a time when He wasn't.
He's the theme of redemption's song.
He was born, and yet uncreated;
He existed before He was man.

In the fullness of time God sent Him
To fulfill His eternal plan.
He created the star that announced His birth
And the tree He was nailed upon.
He suffered and died as our Savior
To reconcile sinful man.

There's no greater gift this Christmas
Than the One that hung on a tree,
Then rose from the grave triumphant
For all the World to see.
He's the reason we celebrate Christmas;
He's our hope for the days ahead.
He's our shelter when storms assail us;
He's with us wherever we're led.

So take time this busy season
To say, "Jesus, I praise your name.
Your presence is the greatest present
And your name is the greatest name!"

Christ's First Greeting

While in the womb, as yet unborn,
This baby leaped for joy.
His spirit sensed his Savior,
God's gift of life, His boy.

Before his eyes were opened,
His spirit recognized
That God was now incarnate,
As prophet's prophesied.

Yes, John would grow to be the voice:
"Prepare, prepare the way!"
The other grew to be the Christ
Who said, "I am the way."

Thank God their mothers understood
God's love for fallen man.
Each babe would play a vital role
In God's eternal plan.

But what if they'd aborted
The lives of these two babes?!
There'd be no Christmas season,
And man would be sin's slave.

A Child Was Born

A child was born; a Son was given,
God's awesome gift sent down from heaven.
He came to bear men's sin and shame.
God's spotless Lamb for us was slain.

Now all who place their faith in Him
Will find deliverance from their sin.
He came to crush the serpent's head
And set men free from fear and dread.

Ascended now to God's right hand,
He has all power at His command.
Nothing's impossible for God.
Our victory is through His blood.

One day, and soon, He will return
For all who look—for those who yearn.
And then for all eternity
I'll worship Him who died for me.

Higher and Higher

Higher and higher, we lift you,
Jesus exalted Son.
No other name is worthy of praise;
Yours is the only one.

We give you glory and honor;
We magnify your name.
You are the Lamb, the great "I Am,"
Forevermore the same.

Risen, exalted, Redeemer;
Almighty God most high,
Nothing on earth can equal your worth.
We lift your name on high.

Oh, for the words to describe you!
Oh, for a way to express
Your mighty power and glory;
Your awesome holiness!

Awaken My Heart

Awaken my heart
As you waken the dawn.
Lord, let your light rise on me.
Turn my night into day
And my blindness to sight,
More of your glory to see.

Your mercies are new every morning.
Yesterday's over and gone.
Come, Lord, today.
Teach me your way.
Lord, for your presence I long.

I Am An Addict

I am an addict,
But I'm not ashamed.
I'm hooked on your presence;
In love with your name.

New every morning
The cravings begin
To know you more deeply,
My Savior and King.

Increase my demand, Lord,
And meet my supply.
Show me your glory!
This is my cry.

I have no desire, Lord,
To ever be free.
I'm bound and addicted
By your love for me.

Lord, Come!

Lord, come in your glory!
Lord, come in your grace!
Lord, come in your mercy!
Come dwell in this place.

Lord, pour out your Spirit;
Descend from on high.
A fresh visitation, Lord!
This is our cry.

Without you we're helpless.
We labor in vain.
Lord, grant us your presence;
Revive us again!

I Make My Boast

I make my boast in Christ alone.
His death brought life to me.
God's justice met, my sin erased;
Now reconciled and free.

No sacrifice, no offering,
Can gain me favor with my King.
His blood: my all sufficiency.
My all, my everything is He.

You're My Well

You're my well from which I draw,
My rock on which I stand,
My anchor in the storm—
The strength of my right hand.

You're my shield when in the fight,
You're my sword against the foe,
You're my wisdom day by day—
You're the greatest friend I know.

I Have No Frankincense

I have no frankincense or gold
To bring to you, my King,
But what I have I freely give:
My all, my everything.

No longer in a manger,
But now upon His throne.
Jesus, my King and Savior,
I worship you alone.

He Listens to the Sound

He listens to the sound
Of the roaring of the sea;
The thunder of the heavens;
The buzzing of the bee.

The noise of children playing;
The sounds of city life;
The salesman and the preacher;
The arguments and strife.

But there's one sound He loves to hear,
A sound for which He craves:
The lifting up of voices
In gratitude and praise!

Come, Holy Spirit!

Come, Holy Spirit!
Come, welcome guest!
Without your presence,
We're like the rest.

Needy and helpless,
Living alone;
Orphans abandoned,
Having no home.

Jesus, you promised
One in your place.
So come, Holy Spirit!
Come take your place!

Oh, the Love!

I was bound by sin's dominion, like a slave; it mastered me.
Then God's love, so rich in mercy, sent His Son to die for me!
Oh, the love that drove those nails in, nails in Him instead of me!
All my sin was laid upon Him; guilty, yet He pardoned me.

I am His, yes, His forever; purchased by His blood alone.
Living now to bring Him pleasure; Jesus Christ my cornerstone.
Let me not forget your mercy and your love revealed to me.
Selfless love that drove those nails in, nails in Him instead of me.

Oh, the love that drove those nails in, nails in Him instead of me!
May I never cease to serve Him, the almighty trinity.
God the Father, Son, and Spirit; I will never comprehend
How for me, a wretched sinner, I by grace could be your friend.

Time will one day be forgotten and eternity begin.
There before your throne I'll worship you my Savior King.
Lamb of God, your wounds forever will recall God's love for me,
Selfless love that drove those nails in, nails in Him instead of me.

(*Tune:* Here is Love. *Robert Lowry 1826-99*)

Better Than the Blood of Abel

Better than the blood of Abel,
The blood of Jesus speaks to me.
Not with words of accusation,
But of life and liberty.

All the blood of sacred offerings
Never could for sin atone.
Only by the blood of Jesus
Can a man be born-again.

Greater than the sin of Adam,
The blood of Jesus testified.
God's demand for righteous justice
Through the cross was satisfied.

Greater than the power of evil,
We can walk in victory.
Sin and Satan's power defeated
Through the blood of Calvary.

Greater than the law of Moses,
Past the veil man could not go.
Now by grace the way is open.
We can enter, white as snow.

Beyond Human Understanding

Beyond the realm of human understanding,
In light so pure no mortal eye can see,
There is a throne eternal in the heavens;
A King unrivaled in His majesty.

Who Is this One so awesome, so amazing,
Who made the world and calls the stars by name,
Yet left His throne to die as my Redeemer;
Poured out His blood for all my sin and shame?

I'll never know the agony He suffered
As nails were driven through His hands and feet.
The cursing crowds, the blasphemies they uttered;
Yet He, God's Lamb, became our mercy seat.

Then from the cross He cried out: "It is finished!"
God's justice He forever satisfied.
On Him were laid my sins and my transgressions,
That all could know by grace we're justified.

There in the grave they laid the Prince of Glory,
The hosts of hell convinced they'd had their way.
But Christ arose, the veil He tore forever;
O'er Satan's power He triumphed on that day.

Oh, what a King! Oh, what an awesome Savior!
That He would wash and claim us as His own;
Call us His bride and He our glorious Bridegroom,
Forevermore to reign with Him alone.

And one day soon He'll come in radiant splendor,
Our conquering King, the nations to reclaim.
And every king and kingdom will behold Him,
The risen Lamb; Christ Jesus is His name.

Then all the earth will tremble at His presence
As He returns to take His rightful place.
And we His people will rejoice to see Him
And worship Him for His amazing grace.

(*Tune:* I Cannot Tell Why He Who Angels Worship. *O Danny Boy*)

Jesus, Our Glorious Majesty

Conceived without the seed of man,
God chose a virgin for His plan.
The One who made the heaven and earth,
She carried in her womb till birth.

Man can't explain this mystery:
That God took on humanity.
Today we celebrate His birth,
Yet more than that—His endless worth.

No longer in a manger laid,
Or on the cross, or in the grave.
Today He reigns eternally;
Jesus our glorious Majesty.

He promised to return one day—
Not as a babe on Christmas day,
But in His awesome power and might;
In flaming fire ready to fight.

The kingdoms of this world He'll claim.
Then over all He'll rule and reign.
Then all the world His power will see,
Jesus our glorious Majesty.

God Almighty Without Equal

God Almighty, without equal;
Great Creator, Majesty;
Father, Son, and Holy Spirit;
Three in one and one in three.
Through the blood of Christ our Savior,
By God's grace you've set us free.
Lord, I lift my hands in worship
For the love you've shown to me.

Now a debtor, Lord, forever;
Take my life and let it be
One of service to your kingdom,
One of love and purity.
I am yours and yours forever,
Purchased by your blood alone.
Let me live to bring you pleasure
Till at last you take me home.

Through your death and resurrection,
You have won the victory.
Principalities and powers
Must forever yield to thee.
King of Glory, Lord of Battle,
Soldiers of the cross are we!
Lord, advance your kingdom through us
Till at last your face we see.

Jesus

His Birth - Irrefutable
His Nature - Incorruptible
His Love - Irresistible
His Mercy - Unbelievable
His Grace - Incomprehensible
His Justice - Unquestionable
His Knowledge - Inscrutable
His Wisdom - Unfathomable
His Power - Unexplainable
His Death - Unquestionable
His Sacrifice - Acceptable
His Visage - Unrecognizable
His Suffering - Inconceivable
His Ascension - Undeniable
His Kingdom - Unconquerable.
His Judgement - Indisputable
His Forgiveness - Unmeritable
His Glory - Indescribable
His Presence - Irreplaceable
His Purpose - Immutable
His Return - Unstoppable

Jesus Was:

Born to fulfill God's word to man
Born to reveal the Father's plan
"Born to be King" was his decree
Born to set the prisoners free

Born to be God's spotless Lamb
Born to die for sinful man
Born to bruise the serpent's head
Born to rise up from the dead

Born to break the chains of sin
Born to make men whole again
Born to be the light of day
Born to show to all the way

Born to heal man's broken heart
Born to give, his peace impart
Born to reign in majesty
Born to rule eternally

Born to return again one day
Born to take his bride away
Born this blessed hope to give
Born that we with Him shall live

That's what Christmas means to me
Love, Joy, Peace, ETERNALLY!

Transcendent

Transcendent in every way;
The heavens forever display
   How great thou art!

Eternal unchangeable King,
   Ruler of everything,
The earth is your footstool;
The heavens your throne.

Lord God Almighty,
By your blood alone
You saved us, redeemed us,
And called us your own.

How great thou art!

Jesus, you are
And will ever be
The one that we worship,
Our great Majesty.

How great thou art!
How great thou art!

Upon the Throne

Upon the throne,
Clothed in majesty,
The Lamb of God:
He reigns eternally.

The great Creator,
Our Lord and Savior,
Has washed us from our sins
And set us free.

His foes defeated,
With Him we're seated
Above all powers and principalities;
The name of Jesus has all authority.

So, let your church arise,
And in His name
The ground on which we tread
For Him we claim.

"Your kingdom come!" our cry.
Our lives we will deny,
Your name to magnify;
Jesus our King.

Exalt His Name

Exalt His name with me:
Jesus, our Majesty!
The Lamb who came to die,
Now risen, exalted high.

There is
No greater name.
Let heaven and earth proclaim
That He is Lord.

From north and south,
From east and west,
They come with one desire:
To glorify God's Son!

From Every Tribe and Nation

From every tribe and nation,
From every tongue and race,
We'll bow in adoration
Before His throne of grace.

We'll sing our hallelujahs
To Christ our risen Lord.
Heaven's thunder will be silenced
By our combined applaud.

We'll praise Him for His mercy
And unrelenting love,
And how He died to save us
And washed us in His blood.

We'll sing the song of Moses,
Give glory to the Lamb
And worship Him, the Prince of Peace,
Our God, Immanuel.

Holy, Holy, Holy

Holy, holy, holy,
Is the risen Lamb;
God Almighty, God Eternal,
God Immanuel.

With your blood you washed us,
God's wrath satisfied.
From sin's kingdom freed us;
By grace justified.

Cherubim and seraphim
In your presence fall.
By your glory awestruck;
On your name they call.

Jesus, Jesus, Jesus,
Worthy is your name!
Matchless is your power;
Endless is your reign.

Every tribe and nation,
Every tongue and race,
Tremble at your presence;
Revel in your grace.

Things Seem to be Falling Apart

Things seem to be falling apart,
But really, they're falling into place.
The seasons are in God's control.
He rules with a smile on His face.

He's told us just what to expect.
There's no need to worry or fear.
The birth-pangs are hastening now;
The time of His coming draws near.

Look up, your redemption draws nigh!
Our bridegroom is seeking His bride.
Make sure you are ready and dressed,
Your lamp full of oil by your side.

Some will not hearken His warnings;
Delay, thinking they know the time.
Their love will begin to wax cold.
He'll say, "They are no friend of mine."

Today is the day to repent.
Lay aside the weights that restrain.
Get back in the race; His forgiveness embrace.
You'll find you have not run in vain.

I Can't Begin to Fathom

I can't begin to fathom
What it will be like to see
The King in all His beauty
And all His majesty!

The glory of His splendor
Outshines the noonday sun.
The fragrance of His presence
Just beckons me to come.

And there before the maker
Of heaven and earth, I'll call
And worship Him forever,
My greatest friend of all.

Father, You Came Running

Father, you came running
When I still smelled like the swine.
You wrapped your arms around me
And cried, "This child of mine!"
You smothered me with kisses,
While held in your embrace.
You dressed me in the best of robes
And hired a band to play.

You let me know beyond all doubt
My sins were wiped away.
The ring and shoes you gave me
Spoke volumes, Lord, to me;
I'm not your slave.
Your son am I.
By grace, restored to thee.

I Saw His Arms Extended

I saw His arms extended;
I heard Him calling: "Come!"
I found myself in motion
    As He began to run.

He wrapped His arms around me
And kissed my tear-stained face,
And instantly my life was changed
    By His amazing grace!

Lord, there's no better feeling,
No greater place to be,
Than in the blood-stained hands of Him
    Who died to set me free!

I Tried to No Avail

I tried to no avail
To enter through the veil.
I longed to meet my Savior face to face.
The Law said I would die
If I should even try,

But then I heard of God's amazing grace.
Sin's penalty was paid when all my sins were laid
Upon God's spotless Lamb, His only Son;
When He rose from the grave
The veil was rent to pave
A way for me.

So now, by blood alone,
I've access to His throne.
My Lord has made a way
For you and me.

Everything We Need, You Are

Everything we need, you are.
Everything you are, we need.
No one else can take your place.
For your presence, Lord, we plead.

You alone can satisfy;
We were made to worship you.
You're the answer to our cry;
Holy, faithful, kind, and true.

Father of Eternity,
Source of every living thing,
Holiness and love entwined;
Of your praise we'll ever sing.

For our sins your blood atoned.
Crucified, then left for dead.
Then out of the grave you rose,
Having bruised the serpent's head.

Now eternally you reign;
Of your kingdom there's no end.
Righteousness and peace and joy;
In your presence we will spend.

Always mindful of your love,
Love that saved a wretch like me,
Ever mindful of those wounds
And the price you paid for me.

Amazing Grace

To think that heaven's eternal throne
Is called the throne of grace!
That Christ in all His majesty
Left heaven to take my place.

Jesus, you satisfied God's wrath.
Justice is now complete.
Mercy and grace you gave to me,
So God and I could meet!

Spirit of grace, I will not spurn
All that you've done for me.
Your grace provides the power to live
In total victory.

Amazing grace! I'll ever sing
When e'er I think of you;
My God, my Savior, Shepherd King,
I love and worship you.

†

Amazing grace! How sweet the sound
That saved a wretch like me.
It cost the Son of God His life
To bring that grace to me.

The Greatest Gift

A virgin would conceive, the prophet cried.
But as the years went by, the promise died.
Then in the fullness of God's perfect time,
A son was born through David's royal line.

His mother Mary, not yet wed,
Gave birth while in a cattle shed.
Joseph was told His name would be
Jesus! (Now known through history.)

He grew in wisdom—stature too—
Confounding those who thought they knew.
Anointed with the Spirit's power,
He healed the sick, made demons cower

He railed against the Pharisee
And made the eyes of blind to see.
He cleansed the lepers, raised the dead
And called Himself the living Bread.

And then because of jealousy,
They crucified Him on a tree.
Three days He lay in burial clothes,
Then from the grave His body rose!

While in the grave, He did proclaim
His triumph over Hell's domain.
O grave, where is your victory?
O'er death and hell "I hold the key!"

Now seated high on heaven's throne,
He longs for us to make Him known.
And so He poured His Spirit forth,
From East to West, from South to North.

Empowering those His bride to be
To witness with authority.
This Christmas season share His love,
The gift of LIFE from heaven above.

There is no greater gift to share
With everyone and everywhere.
He's coming back, not as He came,
But as a King to rule and reign.

Be ready should He come today.
Ask; He'll wash your sins away.

Worthy is the Lamb

Stand to your feet and magnify.
Lift up your hands and glorify
The Son of God who came to die;
Jesus, the Lamb of God.

Worthy the Lamb whose blood was shed;
Raised by God's Spirit from the dead;
The One whose name the demon's dread;
Jesus, the Lamb of God.

Exalt the One who cannot lie,
The One to whom the heaven's cry
Holy, holy, Lord most high!
Jesus, the Lamb of God.

Worthy is the Lamb!
Worthy is the Lamb!
God Almighty, great "I Am."
Worthy is the Lamb!

In Honor of the King

Would everybody rise
In honor of the King!
His royal Majesty is here;
The Lord of everything.

You promised to be with us,
We have your guarantee:
Where two or three are gathered,
That's where you said you'd be.

So, welcome, welcome, welcome!
Your presence, Lord, we crave.
The Lamb who died, then rose again,
Triumphant o'er the grave.

Your power has not abated.
Your glory, Lord, make known.
The earth is but your footstool;
The heavens are your throne.

Your kingdom come, Lord Jesus!
Your will be done on earth.
To every tribe and nation,
Reveal your matchless worth.

Join Us

Joined here in assembly,
Every stone in place,
Here from every nation
Kindred, tribe and race.

Jesus, we your temple
Sacrifices bring.
Grateful hearts as altars,
Worshipping our King.

We are all united
By your blood alone;
Gathered here in worship,
Bowed before your throne.

You alone are worthy.
Holy hands we raise;
Yielded lives we offer;
This our highest praise.

Lord increase our vision
To exalt your name.
To advance your kingdom,
This our only aim.

And when life is over,
These words let us hear:
Well done, faithful servant.
You are welcome here.

We Stand in Awe

We stand in awe
Of your divine allure
And worship you,
The One our hearts adore.

The heavens declare
Your might and majesty.
But greater still,
Your blood speaks life to me.

A debtor now
To your amazing grace;
Your love and mercy
Brought us face to face.

Almighty Father,
Son and Spirit too,
We lift our hearts
And voice to worship you.

Now and forever
We will glorify
The risen Lamb;
Jesus, we magnify.

Pursue Your Foes

Pursue your foes, Almighty God most high.
Lift up your voice and sound the battle cry!
Take up your bow and let your arrows fly.
Disrupt their goals and let their purpose die.

Your kingdom come, our God, our Majesty.
Let heaven and earth your awesome glory see.
Then raise your banner, let the whole earth see
Earth's kings and kingdoms bow on bended knee
Declaring you have won the victory!

From North and South

From north and south, from east and west they come;
From every tribe and nation, from every race and tongue,
United by one passion, to glorify the Lamb.
They bow in awestruck wonder before the great "I Am."
And then what sounds like thunder, they stand in unison
To worship Jesus Christ the Lamb, the Father's glorious Son:
All hail, King Jesus! All hail, Eternal King!
With hearts and hands washed by your blood
Your praise we'll ever sing!

There's Only One Reason

There's only one reason,
And that's why we came
To glorify Jesus,
To exalt His name.

No other is worthy
But Jesus alone;
Our Savior and healer,
The Lamb on the throne.

All glory and honor
To His majesty.
His kingdom forever
And ever will be.

Trinity

He holds the nations in His hands
Like tiny seeds of rice or sand.
Such is His awesome might and majesty.
His throne is in the heavens above;
His footstool is the earth. His love
No other king can match.

His sovereignty?

Like vessels in the potter's hand
He forms the nations small or grand.
Yet He alone decrees their destiny.
There is no limit to His power.
One thousand years is but one hour.
His kingdom reigns through all eternity.

The Father, Son, and Spirit agree;
Three in one, yet one in three;
Together: God,
The Trinity.

To Him Alone

Above all kings and kingdoms;
Above all thrones, dominions;
Above all powers and principalities;
Above all names and nations;
Above all man's inventions;
Above all man's intentions;
Above all arts expressions
And all earth's institutions,
There's a name that transcends all of these—
A name that brings all others to their knees.

His name is Jesus,
The greatest name of all;
The risen Lamb, the great "I Am,"
Now seated on His throne.

So, magnify with me
The Lamb of Calvary.
Glory and honor be
To Him alone.

God Almighty

God almighty, Lord of glory,
Awesome is your name!
You have taken your great power
And begun to reign.

Nations tremble at your presence;
Demons fear and flee.
Mountain's melt like wax before you,
God our Majesty.

Lamb of God,
Redemption's story;
Yours the kingdom,
Power and glory.

By your blood
You cleansed and set us free.
We will worship you
Eternally.

In Your Presence

In your presence, Lord,
Darkness cannot hide; sin cannot abide.
Night turns into day;
Problems flee away.

In your presence, Lord,
Nations rise and fall
At your beck and call;
In your presence, Lord.

Everyone will bend their knee.
There's no place I'd rather be
Than in your company.
There is nothing like your presence, Lord.

He's the King

He's the King, the conqueror of heaven.
He's the mighty God of battle too.
He's the captain of the hosts of heaven.
He's the one who rent the veil in two.

He's the Lamb who gave His life to save us,
Shed His blood to break sin's tyranny.
All the powers of darkness could not hold Him.
He arose and left the grave empty.

He is Jesus Christ, the mighty master;
Son of God and also Son of Man.
He's the Lion of the tribe of Judah.
There's no other like the great "I Am."

Stand to your feet and give Him honor.
Raise your voice and give Him praise!
Lift your hands in full surrender
To our God, Ancient of Days.

Awesome King

Awesome King, we give you glory.
History reveals your story.
By your word you birthed the world we see;
Formed the stars and every galaxy.

Uncreated, God eternal, changeless,
Faultless, without equal;
Who compares to your great majesty?
Holy, righteous, merciful . . .

Faithful, gracious, wonderful;
Jesus, you are all and more to me.
Son of God and Son of Man,
You fulfilled redemption's plan,

Shed your blood and died to set me free.
Now by grace and grace alone
You've prepared for me a home,
To live with you for all eternity.

Abba, Father!

"Abba, Father!" Hear my cry
For more and more of you.

You said if I ask for bread
You'd not give a stone instead,
And to your word
I know you will be true.

So here I stand with open hand;
Your Spirit I desire.
Come, Heavenly Flame—in Jesus' name—
And set my heart on fire!

I Make My Boast

I make my boast in Christ alone.
His death brought life to me.
God's justice met, my sin erased;
Now reconciled and free.

No sacrifice or offering
Could gain me favor with my King.
His blood is my sufficiency.
My all, my everything is He.

The old has passed;
The new begun.
In Christ I stand,
God's risen Son.

Manifest Yourself to Us

Manifest yourself to us;
Your glory let us see.
The glory of your presence
In all your majesty.

Reveal to us your splendor,
Your awesome holiness,
Your wisdom, love and mercy,
Your grace and faithfulness.

Then we in turn will worship
According to your worth.
One family and one nation
Redeemed throughout the earth.

Your blood is what unites us.
Your grace has set us free.
To you alone, Lord Jesus,
All praise and glory be.

Condemned to Die

Condemned to die by love's royal decree;
Guilty as charged, I had no other plea.
God's longing was for me to justify,
But justice also had an equal cry.

To reconcile the two in one,
God sacrificed His only Son.
His law upheld; His love revealed;
My sinful state could now be healed.

Love drove the nails in,
Love drove the nails,
Into His hands and feet.
Love drove the nails, so God and man could meet.

There was no other way;
God's love
Was on display.
He drove the nails in.

God of Nations

God of nations, Sovereign King,
Mighty Lord of everything,
By the power of your decrees,
You determine destinies.
Awesome ruler over all,
By your hand we rise or fall.

Lord revive us, cleanse, renew;
Turn our hearts, Lord, back to you.
God of nations, we entreat;
Hear us from your mercy seat.
From your judgement spare our land.
Change your mind from what you planned.

Lord have mercy! Hear our cry; save us, Lord, or else we die.
We deserve your wrath and more; spare our land, we implore.
God of nations, by your grace, gathered here from every race.
Let your light of liberty testify to none but thee.

Rise in power, your name defend; all opposing forces end.
Great desire of nations, come. Unify us; make us one.
God of nations, let us be ever conscious, Lord, of thee.
From the north, south, east, or west,
Let our land be truly blessed.

Every day and every hour
Show us, Lord, your awesome power.
You alone, Lord, is our cry.
Only You can satisfy.

To Christ Our King

To Christ our King we pledge our lives;
By life or death, a sacrifice.
We will not bend or bow the knee
To any other majesty.

No other king gave up his throne,
Laid down his life to save his own.
The Father's wrath was satisfied.
By faith through Christ we're justified.

His Spirit now our constant guide,
Empowering us from every side.
His gifts can meet man's every need,
Save, heal, restore, and intercede.

Empowered by grace and grace alone,
No turning back; we will press on
His kingdom's purpose to fulfill.
Our sole desire: to do His will.

Our goal completed, we will see
Our King in all his majesty.
No crown can ever take His place
And His approving, smiling face.

God's Priceless Gift

God's priceless gift, one single light,
He placed upon the tree.
The Father's love was there displayed
For all the world to see.

It all began when angels sang
Above the skies of Bethlehem.
Joy to the earth and peace to men!
A Savior's born—God's gift to man!

Born for one reason: born to die,
Sinners to save—like you and I.
And so the Christmas tree we know
Began so many years ago.

Oh, by the way, the gift God gave
They crucified, laid in the grave.
But darkness can't dispel the light;
He conquered death to give us life.

When you exchange your gifts this year,
God's greatest gift is still right here—
To comfort, guide, forgive, and bless—
Jesus, our gift of righteousness.

Another Conference

To some, another conference is addictive—like a drug.
They make it their priority, while other things they shrug.
They sing, then sit and listen to their favorite "man of God,"
Feeding of his messages as if they were a hog.

No sooner do they return to friends and family,
Than they're inquiring when another conference will be.
You see, they live to get their fix, a type of spiritual high.
They've never learned to study and pray; without a fix they die.

While conferences may do some good, they often interfere
With what it means to daily seek their God throughout the year.
Now please don't criticize me; I've done the conference tour—
A few days here, a few days there—it's endless to be sure.

Meanwhile the local pastors are the ones we need to thank.
Like parents of a needy child, they bathe, feed, love and spank.
Yes, their reward will be immense, as well you might agree.
Yet their applause will have to wait until eternity.

Let This Cup Pass

He was born for one reason: to die for our sin.
God's Lamb was born perfect without and within.
His mission on earth was to please God above
And tell every man of God's awesome love.

He knew in the end that He'd have to die,
And told his disciples the real reason why.
They didn't understand and paid little heed.
It didn't make sense, and they failed to believe.

But then came the night before Passover Day,
When Jesus went to the garden to pray.
There the sin of the world seemed to tear Him apart,
And He thought He would die from the pain in His heart.

"My soul's greatly grieved," they all heard Him say.
His sweat was like blood; He continued to pray,
"If I die right now, Lord, then what of the cross—
Your plan of salvation—will all suffer loss?

So let this cup pass, Lord!
The cross I'll fulfill.
But if there's a way that I don't understand,
Not my will, but yours; my life's in your hand!

We Serve Notice

We serve notice to the powers of darkness:
United in the name of the Lord,
We remind you of the cross of Jesus,
That His blood has more power than the sword.

Jesus bruised your head, as was promised,
When He rose from the grave that day,
And stripped all your might and power—
Your defeat put on full display.

We've been given almighty power:
The blood, the Word, and His name!
No weapon can stand against us
When we lift our voice and proclaim:

"The Lord rebuke you, Satan,
In Jesus mighty name!"
Your kingdom come, Lord Jesus.
The Earth is your domain.

One Day

One day the clouds will part and we will see
Our King in all His glorious majesty.
We'll sing the song of Moses and the Lamb,
Jesus, almighty God, the great "I Am."

The one who is, and was, and yet will be
Worthy of honor, praise, eternally.
And every knee will bow, from every tribe and race.
And every tongue will sing, "Amazing Grace!"

Thank You

I've come to say, "Thank you,"
To lift up your name.
I've come to say, "Jesus,
I'm so glad you came!"

You showed us the Father,
His love and His grace,
Then showed us His mercy
And died in our place.

You made us your dwelling;
What more can I say?
That Christ dwells within me
By night and by day.

My life is complete now.
New purpose you gave:
To live for you only
And others to save.

You Are the One

You are the one who created the heavens.
You made the earth and the sea.
Your throne alone stands without equal.
Great is your majesty.

You have the power to call forth the morning.
You set the course for the sun.
You place the smile on the face of a child.
You cause the rivers to run.

You gild the fields with the dew of the morning.
You call the stars by their name.
You never change, you're constant, eternal;
Always and ever the same.

You captured my heart by your grace, so amazing.
Your blood washed my sins away.
Your love fills the void the world had created.
You are the joy of my day.

The Ultimate King

The ultimate King,
In His ultimate love,
Paid the ultimate price for me.
He surrendered His throne as ruler of all
To suffer and die on a tree.

His ultimate grace is sufficient
For my ultimate sin and shame.
Now the ultimate gift
—Eternal life—
Links me to His ultimate name.

The Place Where Your Glory Dwells

The place where your glory dwells,
The place of your majesty,
The place of your presence, Lord,
That's where I long to be.

But sin cannot enter,
And pride has no place.
It's only your mercy;
I'm drawn by your grace.

No merit of mine, Lord;
Through your blood alone
I enter your presence
To stand at your throne.

I'll worship before you;
I'll gaze and adore.
The longer I'm with you,
I hunger for more.

I Stand in Fascination

I stand in fascination, in awe of your creation,
Before the one who formed the earth and sea.
Defying explanation, the father of creation,
   Transcends all others in supremacy.

Almighty God eternal, your glory has no equal.
The heavens declare your matchless majesty.
But what is more amazing comes the revelation
In love you gave your son to die for me.

His blood bought my redemption and reconciliation;
A sinner saved for all the world to see.
In deep appreciation, in love and adoration,
I'll praise your name throughout eternity.

Amazing Grace

Amazing grace, forever mine;
Forgiven now and free.
A slave to sin, but now at last
His slave I'll ever be.

One day I'll gaze upon His face,
My Savior and my King.
I'll bow before His mercy-seat,
And this is what I'll sing:

"Amazing grace; how sweet the sound
That saved a wretch like me!
I once was lost, but now I'm found.
Was blind, but now I see."

Oh, may I not despise that grace
That set this captive free.
Give me a hatred for all sin,
Lord. Place your fear in me.

You Make the Sun

You make the sun to rise every morning,
Flooding the earth with light.
You make the snow to fall in the winter,
Covering the earth in white.

You cause the flowers to bloom in the springtime,
Colors of every hue.
You draw us, Lord, by your Spirit of grace,
Causing a hunger for you.

From you, and through you, and to you are all things;
Everything you hold in place.
One day I'll stand in wonder before you,
There to behold your face.

They Crucified God's Only Son

They crucified God's only son.
They drove the nails in one by one.
They plucked his beard, spat in his face;
They whipped his back, beat on his head,
Then left Him on the cross as dead.
No spoken word, no writer's pen
Can tell the pain, the agony
That Jesus felt upon that tree.

Amazing grace came at a price;
God's son became sin's sacrifice.
Yes, He was wounded there for me
To break sin's chains and set me free.
One day I'll gaze into His face,
Then kneel before His throne of grace
And praise His name forevermore—
And worship, worship, and adore.

Forbidden to Enter

Forbidden to enter,
It's no longer true.
The veil that divided,
Is now torn in two.
No curtain between us.
Your grace welcomes all
To stand in your presence,
On your name to call.

A sinner no longer,
Your blood cleanses me.
With boldness I enter,
Forgiven and free.
The Day of Atonement
forever complete.
No longer a stranger
At your mercy seat.

I Came to Fulfill

Have you ever considered the price Jesus paid,
 The agony suffered when he was betrayed?
 It was there in the garden the battle began.
If He should die there then what of God's plan?

He came with one purpose and that was to die,
 Like the brazen serpent that Moses held high.
 But such was His pain in the garden that night,
 That God sent an angel to strengthen His might.

He prayed so intently His sweat looked like blood.
 And this is where He has been misunderstood.
 My Lord wasn't selfishly thinking that He
Could escape from the cross; He was thinking of me.

I came for one reason to die for man's sin
 If I perish now there's no sin offering!
 Yet nevertheless, He yielded His will.
 Your purpose, my God, I came to fulfill.

When You've Tried Every High

When you've tried every high,
Yet you find you're so low
That you just want to die
Cause you've no place to go,
Let me tell you, my friend,
That God understands.
Just turn from you sin;
Place your life in His hands.

He'll cleanse and restore you.
The price has been paid.
Yes, He shed His blood,
Then He rose from the grave.
He's waiting for you to say,
"Jesus, I come.
Wash me and make me
Your daughter or son."

You'll never regret
The decision you make
To reach out to God;
Leave the past in your wake.

The King of Love

The King of love, the King of grace,
The King of every tribe and race.
The King of heaven and earth below
Sent us His son, His love to show.

But Satan sought to thwart God's plan
And crucified God's spotless Lamb.
But Satan's plan forever caved;
The Son of God rose from the grave!

And now He reigns eternally,
The King who gave His life for me.
Now I can stand on holy ground;
My righteousness in Him is found.

From Every Tribe and Nation

From every tribe and nation, from every tongue and race,
We're here in celebration of your amazing grace.
Your blood has paid our ransom—no longer bound; now free!
Once aliens and orphans, now one vast family.

Once rejected; now accepted. Once blind, but now we see.
Once aimlessly we wandered. Now you're our destiny.
Our sacrifice of worship, we will forever bring
To you, Jesus our Savior, our great eternal King.

Born to Die

Born to die, but then to reign.
Born God's Lamb, for sinners slain.
Born to bruise the serpent's head.
From the grave, rose from the dead.

Tore the veil from head to toe;
There by faith we too can go.
Boldly at God's throne to stand,
Bringing nothing in our hand.

Saved by grace and grace alone;
Fully did His blood atone.
There is nothing man can add.
It would lead us all to brag.

Christ alone has paid the price;
He our living sacrifice.

Almighty God

Almighty God, Creator King,
Our sacrifice of praise we bring.
You are awesome! You are awesome!
No one on earth or heaven above
Can match your grace and endless love.
Loving Father! Loving Father!
God Almighty! God Almighty! God Almighty!

Jesus our great victorious Lamb,
Great Son of God and Son of Man,
You forgave us! You forgave us!
God's righteousness you satisfied.
Your blood forever "mercy!" cries.
What a Savior! What a Savior!
Thank you, Jesus. Thank you, Jesus. Thank you, Jesus.
Jesus, you crushed the serpent's head,
Then rose in triumph o'er the dead.
Mighty conqueror! Mighty conqueror!
You hold the keys of death and hell,
Jesus our Lord, Emanuel.
We adore you! We adore you!
You're amazing! You're amazing! You're amazing!

Great King of righteousness and peace,
Your reign will never ever cease.
King eternal! King eternal!
Rulers throughout earth's history
Will bow before your majesty.
Crying, "Worthy!" Crying, "Worthy!"
King of Glory! King of Glory! King of Glory!

(Hymn Tune: Let All Creation Rise and Sing*)*

A Glorious Bride

I read these lines the other day
—they wouldn't let me get away:
"The night is darkest before the morn'.
When the pain is sorest, the child is born."

Through the valley of death He leads us;
A table before us to spread.
In the presence of our enemies
We feast on His wine and bread.

So, never complain 'bout His leading;
His motive is always our best.
In darkness and pain are His methods
That lead us to His peace and to rest.

Diamonds are formed under pressure,
And pearls are from problems made.
Our Savior was marred beyond measure,
The rose from an empty grave.

We are told: For the joy set before Him
He suffered and bled and died;
His sorrow was turned into morning,
And His pain birthed a glorious bride.

Odds & Ends

The Bride & Groom

When God created Adam, He came to realize
That there was no one else around for Adam to fix his eyes.
"It is not good," God said, "For man to be alone.
I'll make for him a helpmate, someone to share his home."

And so he laid man down to sleep and formed a work of art.
He took from Adam's side a rib, from just below his heart.
He fashioned her to be a friend, to walk with side by side,
To love and cherish as his own—indeed, to be his bride.

He didn't take from Adam's head, so he could rule and reign,
Or from his feet to symbolize that she was his domain.
No. God designed the woman to be man's counterpart,
And so He formed her from man's side, to love with all his heart.

Together they were called to serve—God's destiny fulfill—
To find their highest pleasure in obedience to His will.

Father or G_d

The more you get to know someone
The closer you become.
Many start out just as friends
And soon become as one.

Now that's the way God planned it
For God and man to be.
He longs for every person
To join His family.

So why, I ask, do those who boast
Of knowing Him as friend
Refuse to call Him by His name,
Lest they should God offend?

Now doesn't it stand to reason
The closer you become,
That you would call your friend by name
And not a shortened one?

When Jesus came, He broke the rules
Of so-called piety.
Let's face it: He alone could speak
Truth's full reality.

He said, to call God "Father,"
Just like a child would say.
So simple and yet so profound;
Let's leave it just that way.

Then I Awoke

Amazing grace!
How sweet the sound that forced a wretch like me
To leave my sin and take Christ in, for He predestined me?
I could not but refuse His grace, no matter how I may;
My calling and election were beyond my choice that day?
Before all time my God had planned to save my sinful soul.
Some were not chosen, so they say; a few, but not the whole.
Way back before the world began, God wrote a script for me
That I have followed all my life;
God rigged my destiny?

I'd rather choose the God I serve, love Him with all my heart,
Than to be told I'd simply played a pre-determined part.
Then I awoke one day to see that I could spurn God's grace,
That God had given me a choice to choose His awesome grace.
Christ paid the penalty for all and freely bids us come,
Receive the cleansing of His blood and choose Him as our own.
No more a robot, but a son; no longer bound, but free.
To choose the Master that I serve for all eternity.

John Calvin, you're no friend to grace with your theology.
To say that God predestined all; then man can't be guilty.
Men could blame the god who says, "You had no choice at all!
Sin and Satan were decreed way back before the fall."
"No, no!" cried I, "that is not so; you said,
'Choose you this day.'
So I responded to your call to serve, love and obey."

The Fungus Among Us

There's a fungus among us from China's Wuhan.
They say all you need is a jab in the arm.
They promise us peace if we follow their rules:
Wear a mask at all times; keep your kids out of schools.

Make sure you comply or they'll send Fauci by,
And he'll report you to the feared FBI.

So be sure to carry your card at all times!
It shows you've been *vaxxed,* and it sure beats the fines.
Here's hoping this plague will soon pass away
And we will all live to see a new day.

But just when you think this virus is gone,
A new variant soon comes along.
Now, I understand this raises some fear;
To many a sign, that the end is quite near.

Others believe, from the greatest to least,
That taking the jab is the *mark of the beast.*

It's not what goes into the arm that defiles,
But out of the mouth, either curses or smiles.
Now listen my friend, God is still here.
On Him cast your cares, there's no need to fear.

And if for some reason you do pass away
You'll wake up in heaven, to start a new day.

Left or Lost?

A shepherd's role is quite complex, as well you might agree.
If you could walk with him a day, or two, or even three.
Sheep, like no other creature, have a mind all of their own.
Some seem content to simply graze and seldom ever roam,
While others never settle—they are always on the go.
From flock to flock they move about,
Where next you never know.
From time to time they reappear
With tales of greener grass.
They don't commit to serve the flock;
When asked to help, they pass.
Then there are some who grow long horns
And use them day and night.
They're always moving through the flock,
Delighting in a fight.

Some sheep are weak and weary, in constant need of care.
They hang around the shepherd in hope of love and care.
Sheep come in various colors, in sizes large and small.
But to the faithful shepherd, his love includes them all.

Now, please don't get the feeling that all the flock are bad.
The vast majority of them just make the shepherd glad.
One of the great dilemmas that shepherds face today,
Is how to tell if one has left or simply gone astray.
If he should try to search them out, it might be deemed *control*.
But what if they have gone astray? He'll answer for their soul.
So please, if you're not with us, pick up the phone and call.
We'd like to know that you're okay; We want what's best for all.

A Fish Tale

This is a tale about a dear friend —
A preacher, but also a great fisherman.
His passion to fish brought him great delight.
He fished both by day as well as by night.

One night while out fishing, the moon giving light,
He caught something big; it started to fight.
He could tell by the strain that this was some catch!
The battle was on, but who'd win the match?

Despite all his skill, he started to pray.
He couldn't afford to let this get away.
For over an hour it fought for its life.
He thought to himself, "I'll show this to my wife!"

As the fish slowly rose to the edge of the boat
He saw a real trophy and started to gloat.
"This one's not to eat; I'll mount it instead
So all of my friends can see it," he said.

Thrilled and excited, he reach for his net.
His prize within reach, he started to sweat.
He lowered his net towards its huge head,
And *thud!* went the sound as he fell out of bed.

Sometimes We Get Offended

Sometimes we get offended
When things don't go our way.
Instead of yielding, we react
And want to have our say.

And if no one will listen,
We fear we'll lose control.
And so, to keep our image,
We spiritualize the whole.

God's telling me that I should …
Or some similar refrain.
They can't admit to being wrong,
And so, they shift the blame.

But love holds no account of wrong,
But dies to self's demands.
Love seeks what's best for others;
Places all things in God's hands.

The key to having peace, my friend,
Is let God have full sway.
Surrender what you think is best.
Let Jesus have His way.

Can a Horse Change Into ...

Can a horse change into a monkey;
Or a turkey change into a cow;
Can a zebra become a tiger;
Or a giraffe change into a sow?

Can a camel become a kangaroo;
Can an elephant turn into a bat;
Can a tortoise change into a cheetah;
Or a rabbit change into a cat?

Can a goat change into a mouse;
Or a porcupine change to a frog;
Can a weasel become a lama;
Or a snake turn into a dog?

Can a squirrel change into a hedgehog;
Or a mouse turn into a sloth;
Can a bear change into a dolphin;
Or an eagle turn into a moth?

Can an ostrich change into a sparrow;
Or a moose turn into a clam;
Can a peacock change into a donkey;
Or a lizard turn into a lamb?

Such ideas seem quite preposterous;
That an ant can become a rhinoceros,
Or a tiny little chinchilla
Can turn and become a gorilla!

Everything God made for a purpose.
Every one of us is unique.
Aren't you glad we all have noses?
What if we all had beaks?

Girls grow up to be ladies,
And boys grow up to be men.
But the lie the Devil is spreading is
That Sally can change into Ben.

This lie says you'll never be happy
The way you were born to be.
Don't ever believe that the lie is true.
God made you a HE or a SHE.

Now if you're confused by what you've been told,
Ask God and He'll set you free.
Then thank Him for how He has made you,
As perfect as perfect can be.

When Will it All End?

When will it all end?
How long will it be
Until I am found
And finally free?

All day and all night
I'm used and abused.
They treat me like trash,
Like yesterday's news.

Oh, God, if you're real,
Please help me, I pray!
I can't live like this,
Yet can't get away.

My body's in pain.
My mind is confused.
I long to go home;
My captors refuse.

I'm sold everyday.
My wage is more pain.
Consumed by their lust;
They return again.

From city to city,
I'm sold as a slave.
When will it all end?
When will I be saved?

The pain carries on
From night until day.
I'm given no choice.
The men have their way.

I dream, when alone,
The day will soon come
When I'll be set free
And make my way home.

Oh, God, hear my cry!
Have mercy on me.
Forgive me, I pray.
Set my spirit free.

So whether I'm found
Or die as I am,
I'll know that I'm loved
At least by one man.

The Date

If you've ever travelled the world my friend,
You'll know what I say is true:
Each country has its own currency;
We all could name a few.

And on each coin, you'll find a date: the year the coin was struck.
But did you ever stop to think that date got there by luck?
Each date bears testimony of the coming of a king.
It doesn't matter where you live, from New York or Beijing.

King Jesus Christ divided time from BC to AD,
And every coin bears witness to that reality.
The communist, the Muslim, the atheist, the Jew—
Each coin they hold, the date declares: He came to die for you.

Two thousand years have come and gone
Since God sent us His Son.
But fewer years by far remain
For His return to come.

Next time you hold a coin, just think: its date will guarantee
That since Christ came the first time, He'll return for you and me.
Now think of all the coins you've held yet failed to realize
That each recalls the promise that Christ was prophesied.

And so, this Christmas season we celebrate Christ's birth;
God's promise of a Savior whose death revealed your worth.
So why not stop to thank Him for all He's done for you;
For His great love and faithfulness;
For all He's brought you through.

www.ingramcontent.com/pod-product-compliance
Lightning Source LLC
Chambersburg PA
CBHW060536100426
42743CB00009B/1541